Sophia the Supergirl

She Knows How to Fight Dyslexia

Her Secret Power Revealed

The Story of Sophia
How She Became a Super Girl

It Started Not So Long Ago...

The Day Sophia Was Born with a Superpower

With Her Superpower, She Could Create Dancing Pictures in Her Mind

Sophia Also Created Dancing Pictures While Reading Her Favorite Stories

Sophia Became Very Powerful as She grew up. She Learned the Name of Her Pet Max Very Easily

When Sophia Went to School, She Was Very Excited to Talk About Her Dancing Pictures and Max

However, with time, Sophia Realized Reading Became Difficult for Her.

Really?

Didn't She Have the Superpower?

Definitely Yes!

She Had the Superpower to Make Things Dance in her Mind. So, When She Started Writing, the Letters Would Spin. The 'Max' Became 'Xam'.

It Seemed that She Was not Able to Control Her Powers Anymore.

She Became Very Sad, Thinking that She had Lost Her Superpower.

But Did She?

Sophia Wanted to Read to Create More Dancing Pictures in Her Mind and, at the Same Time, Prevent Letters from Dancing

Here Came Her Angel to Help Her.

Angela, Her Favorite Teacher, Knew Her Problem. She Guided Her on How to Control the Superpower with the Mind's Eye.

In fact, Angela Had the Superpower too.

The Mind's Eye Helped Her Stop Letters from Dancing while Make Other Things Dancing Whenever She Wanted.

Mind's Eye Worked Like a Camera, You Take Pictures Only When You Open it.

So, Sophia Decided to Try That Too, And it Worked.

She Learned How to Control Her Mind's Eye and Open it While Playing and Close it While Reading

Now She Could Read, Write Without Any Difficulty, and Create Dancing Pictures Whenever She Wanted

She Could Write 'Max' Instead of 'Xam' Very Easily.

Sophia Also Used Her Superpower to Remember the Spellings.

She Created Funny Stories in Her Mind to Remember How to Spell.

Now Sophia Gets the Full Marks in Her Spelling Test – Thanks to Her Superpower.

She Loves Reading, Writing and Doing Her Homework.

Why Wouldn't She?

Sophia is a Supergirl, After all!

Now You Know Her Secret

Ready to Become a Super Girl?

Take Control of Your Mind's Eye!

Printed in Great Britain
by Amazon